THIS BOOK BELONGS TO:

_____

WELCOME TO ALASKA

Mimi Jones

Dedicated to all the explorers out there.

All rights reserved.
No part of this book may be reproduced in any form or by any means, electronic or mechanical, and no photocopying or recording, unless you have written permission from the author.

ISBN 978-1-958985-27-4

Text copyright © 2024 by Mimi Jones

www.joeysavestheday.com

A Mimi Book

Alaska was purchased from Russia by the United States in 1867.

The name "Alaska" comes from the Aleut word "Alaxsxaq," sometimes spelled "Alyeska." This word means "mainland" or "the great land," referring to the landmass that the Aleuts saw as the main part of their world, where the vast sea meets and crashes against it. The word captures the sheer, rugged majesty of Alaska's expansive landscapes and its integral role in the lives of the indigenous peoples who first named it.

Alaska was the forty-ninth state to join the union.
It officially joined on January 3rd, 1959.

Alaska is a state within the United States; however, it is not physically connected to the contiguous United States. Instead, it shares a border with Canada.

Juneau is the capital of Alaska. It officially became the capital in 1906.

Juneau, Alaska, has an estimated population of 32,227 people.

Alaska is the largest state in the United States.

There are about 731,545 people who reside in the state of Alaska.

Benny Benson, born in Chignik, Alaska on September 12, 1912, created the state flag of Alaska at the age of 14. His design, featuring the Big Dipper and the North Star, won a contest in 1927 and has been the official state flag since Alaska's statehood in 1959.

The Alaska Native Heritage Center in Anchorage is a cultural hub celebrating Alaska's Indigenous peoples. Visitors can explore life-sized village sites, watch traditional dances, and join interactive demos. It's a place to learn about Alaska's Native cultures like the Dene, Iñupiat, and Yup'ik. It's a living showcase of history and heritage.

Instead of counties, Alaska is divided into boroughs.

Alaska has over 20 boroughs, here is a list of 20 them:

Aleutians East	Lake and Peninsula
Anchorage	Matanuska-Susitna
Bristol Bay	North Slope
Denali	Northwest Arctic
Fairbanks North Star	Petersburg
Haines	Sitka
Juneau	Skagway
Kenai Peninsula	Unorganized
Ketchikan Gateway	Wrangell
Kodiak Island	Yakutat

The Klondike Gold Rush stands as a pivotal chapter in the history of Alaska. The 1896 gold discovery in the Klondike region of the Yukon triggered a mass migration of about 100,000 prospectors, all eager to stake their claims and seek their fortunes.

Point Retreat Light is a lighthouse located on Admiralty Island in Alaska. It was built in 1904.

252 Marine Way
Juneau, Alaska

One of the many things Alaska is known for is the Aurora Borealis, also called the Northern Lights. The Aurora Borealis is a beautiful phenomenon where green, purple and red lights seem to dance across the sky.

Alaska has around 100,000 glaciers that cover about 5 percent of the state.

The Alaska state bird is the Willow Ptarmigan. The Willow Ptarmigan is known as a master of camouflage because it turns all white in the winter, and in the warmer months, its coloring turns a mixture of reds and browns.

The Alaska official state flower is the forget-me-not, which comes in shades of blue, pink, purple, white, and yellow.

During the summer months, areas near the Arctic Circle experience the magical phenomenon known as the Midnight Sun. This event occurs when the sun remains visible even after midnight, sometimes shining for 24 hours straight.

Alaska's nickname is The Last Frontier.

PROMISE

Alaska's state motto is North to the Future, which means that Alaska is the land of promise.

The Alaska state flag was flown for the first time on July 9, 1927. The Alaska state flag features 7 gold stars that form the big dipper and one more giant gold star for the north star or the most northern state in the Union.

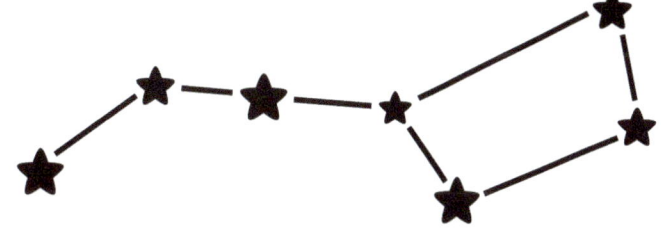

Some things produced in Alaska are hay, dairy, beans, beets, broccoli, potatoes, and cauliflower.

Some animals that inhabit Alaska include river otters, moose, walrus, lynx, arctic fox, mountain goat.

Alaska experiences extreme temperatures. The highest recorded was 100°F n Fort Yukon on June 27, 1915, and the lowest was -80°F in Prospect Creek on January 23, 1971.

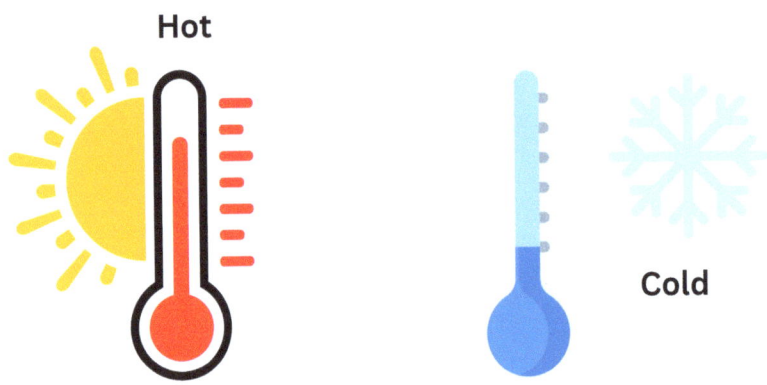

In Alaska dogs like the Alaskan Malamute and Siberian Huskies are used to pull sleds over long distances, even in tough conditions. Sled dogs help with transport and compete in races like the Iditarod.

Pioneer Park is a great place to visit in Fairbanks, Alaska.

2300 Airport Way
Fairbanks, AK 99701

Some features of the park.

Carousel

Canoeing

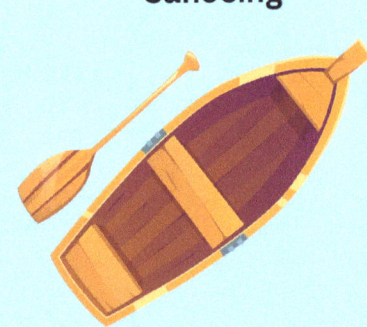

Volleyball

Playground

Biking

Cornhole

Denali National Park in Alaska is a vast wilderness home to North America's tallest peak, Denali. Known for its stunning landscapes, diverse wildlife, and numerous outdoor activities, the park is a paradise for nature lovers and adventurers.

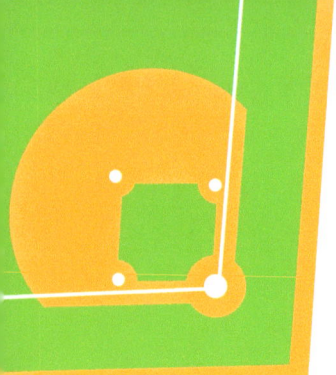

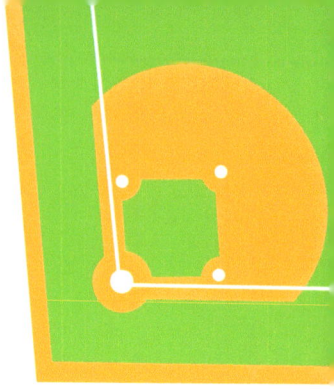

The Chugiak-Eagle River Chinooks are a collegiate summer baseball team based outside Anchorage, Alaska. They compete in the Alaska Baseball League and play home games at Lee Jordan Field in Chugiak.

The South Anchorage Varsity Boys Football team, known as the Wolverines, represents South Anchorage High School in Anchorage, Alaska.

Alaska's totems are carved wooden poles by Indigenous tribes like the Tlingit, Haida, and Tsimshian. They tell stories about clan history, events, or spiritual beliefs through detailed carvings of animals, humans, and mythical beings. These totems preserve the cultural heritage and traditions of Alaska's Native communities.

Can you name these?

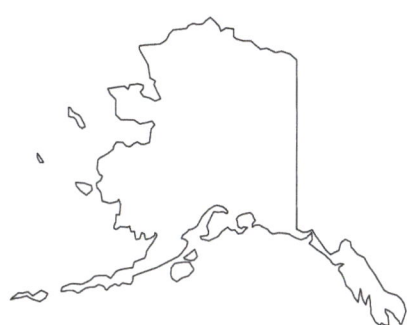

I hope you enjoyed learning about Alaska.

To explore fun facts about the other 49 states, visit my website at www.joeysavestheday.com. You'll also find a wide variety of homeschool resources to support joyful learning at home. If you enjoyed this book, I would be grateful if you left a review. Your feedback truly helps. Thank you for your support!

Check out these other interesting books in the 50 States Fact Books Series!

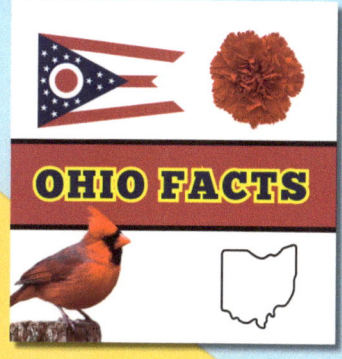

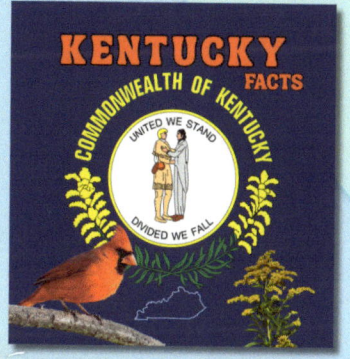

www.mimibooks.com

www.ingramcontent.com/pod-product-compliance
Lightning Source LLC
Chambersburg PA
CBHW040027050426
42453CB00002B/31